# Once Upon a War

## The Memoir of Gertrud Schakat Tammen
### as told to Diana Star Helmer

TITLE I
FEDERAL FUNDED PROGRAM
2012 - 2013

Perfection Learning®

## Dedication

I dedicate this book to my only sibling, my sister Eva Waltraud Schakat Krueger, who became my best friend in adulthood. Without her, I might not have survived. And to future generations, with a plea to do everything possible to avoid wars.

**Image Credits:** Corbis pp. 6, 27, 44; Hulton-Deutsch Collection/Corbis pp. 14 (top), 45; Austrian Archives/Corbis p. 14 (bottom); Zandria Muench Beraldo/Corbis p. 17; Bettmann/Corbis pp. 33, 35

Digital Stock p. 5; National Archives p. 20; PhotoDisc, Inc. pp. 32, 52; United States Holocaust Memorial Museum Photo Archives pp. 37, 38; Photos provided by Gertrud Schakat Tammen cover, pp. 9, 10, 11, 13, 18, 19, 21, 22, 26, 39, 42, 43, 51, 54; Corel p. 41; Library of Congress p. 48; Bundesarchiv Koblenz, Germany p. 56; Some images copyright www.arttoday.com

**Book Design:** Alan D. Stanley
**Cover Design:** Tobi Cunningham

PB ISBN-13: 978-0-7891-5357-9  ISBN-10: 0-7891-5357-2
RLB ISBN-13: 978-0-7807-9736-9  ISBN-10: 0-7807-9736-1

4  5  6  7  PP  13  12  11  10
PPI / 10 / 10

# Table of Contents

# Introduction

Gertrud Schakat Tammen was born in 1931 in northeastern Germany, which was then called East Prussia and is now part of Russia. When the battles of World War II forced Gertrud and her family from their home, Gertrud kept a diary of their travels as they searched for a new life. That diary is included in *Diary of a War Child: The Memoir of Gertrud Schakat Tammen.*

The war drained Germany of its opportunities for young people. So in 1954, after graduating from high school and nurse's training, Mrs. Tammen came to the United States. In Iowa, she worked as a nurse, the job of her dreams.

One day in 1994, Mrs. Tammen was bandaging a patient's foot.

"What do you do for a living?" she asked her patient.

"I write children's books," the young woman answered.

"I kept a diary when I was a girl," said Mrs. Tammen. "I've always wanted it to be a real book."

That is how Mrs. Tammen met Diana Star Helmer, and that is how this book began.

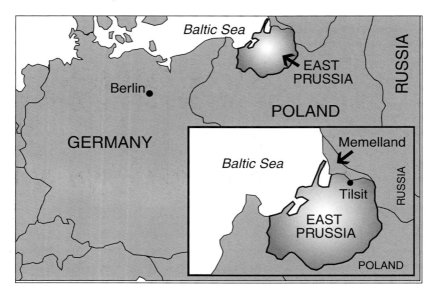

# Chapter 1

# June 22, 1941

I woke up in the middle of the night. My parents were looking out our bedroom window. Something was wrong with the color of the dark.

I heard a blast. It sat me straight up.

The whole house was afraid. It shook, harder and harder. I ran after Mama and Papa into the hall.

"Those are our planes," Papa shouted over the racket. "Those are definitely German planes. Hear how they're headed east?"

"We're attacking Russia." Mama's voice was flat. But her eyes blazed.

Russia! I thought.

Russia was just miles from our town of Tilsit. That's why German planes were flying over us. They almost had to in order to get to Russia.

Mama, Papa, and I scurried barefoot to the door of our spare bedroom. Papa knocked. The two soldiers in there had the only east window in our apartment. It was the only place we could watch the skies.

Almost every family in Tilsit had soldiers staying with them. Ours had lived with us a few weeks now. But I still felt shy going into that room—a room in our own home! I leaned against Mama as we stared out their window into the heavy, red sky.

Slowly, the redness changed. It got softer—more real. Then it turned into a sunrise. It was just like any other day.

I decided to get dressed. But what should I wear? Today was Sunday. We always dressed up on weekends, starting Saturday after school. Papa would read the paper. We'd visit the cousins. Everyone relaxed on weekends.

But who could relax today? Was it safe to go visiting? What were the Russians going to do?

We'd have to wait for the radio to come on. Then we would find out. Unless . . . no, we would find out.

Finally, it was five o'clock. Papa snapped the radio dial. The familiar voice of Dr. Goebbels, our Minister of **Propaganda**, bit through the gray morning light.

We were right. Germany was attacking Russia! Dr. Goebbels reminded us why. German people in Russia needed our help, he said. Russia was a **Communist** state that mistreated people.

"Are those bombs?" Mama interrupted.

I heard the sound too.

"Bombs don't come from the ground," Papa said. He stood up and turned down the radio. "That's *flak* from **antiaircraft** guns. The Russians must be fighting back, and we're shooting at their planes."

The racket changed. Overhead, we heard a whine of engines. Then a slow whistling grew louder and then softer.

"Those are bombs," Papa said.

Mama gripped my shoulder. She almost shoved me out the apartment door in front of her. White-faced neighbors poured out of their apartments, pressing toward the basement.

"Mama?" I whispered on the stairs. "If the fighting comes here, we could go to *Onkel* Ernst's, couldn't we? Tilsit is close to Russia, but Onkel Ernst lives 50 miles away. The Russians couldn't shoot from here to Konigsberg, could they?"

> **Onkel** (OHN-kel) is the German word for "uncle."

Mama put her arm around me.

The chickens in the basement clucked, ruffled, and hopped out the window at the sight of all those people. Then the **air-raid sirens** started. They blew the chickens back into the basement in a squawking cloud.

The sirens didn't stop. They kept blasting and blasting. The sound pushed down on me. It squeezed me until I hunched next to Mama on the laundry room bench.

I can't die, I thought. It is only two days until my birthday. Kids can't get killed before they're ten, can they?

I looked around. Suddenly, it seemed like Sunday. We sat there with strangers and family. Faint sunlight streamed from the high, small windows. It was like church.

At last, the sirens stopped. The flak stopped. Then came a long, steady blast on the siren.

"All clear," Papa said. It seemed like everyone breathed and started talking at once.

"We'd better go see what it looks like," someone said.

We squinted in the outside light. But everything looked all right—just like before. The sun was even shining. That was strange, because I thought I heard thunder.

We went up to our apartment.

At noon, we heard a commotion outside. People outside were calling to people inside. "Hurry! Come see the ships on the river!" We ran to see.

*Russians*. Prisoners! Most of them were barefoot and in their underwear.

I felt safer somehow. The Russians couldn't hurt us if they were our prisoners!

As Papa and I walked back home, he looked up. "Those cannons sure sound like thunder, don't they?" he said.

We ate our Sunday dinner, just like always. The sounds of planes, artillery, and cannons were fading now.

"We're getting deep into Russia," Papa said. "Those cannons are pretty far away."

Mama snorted, "Far away." She took his empty plate.

I listened. All I could hear was the clink of forks, Papa chewing, and a neighbor's footsteps under our open window.

Tired from being up so early, we kissed good night before it was **blackout**. Papa's bare feet and nightshirt made me think of those Russian prisoners.

I liked knowing they were in jail somewhere. I liked knowing they were far away.

# Chapter 2

# July 1941

Air-raid sirens howled all the next day and on my birthday too. But we only heard sirens—no planes or bombs.

Each night, we scurried to the basement—chickens clucking and neighbors talking. We were always back upstairs for the 10 p.m. radio news. Every broadcast reported that Germany had captured more and more Russian cities.

The air alerts stopped after that week. Our two soldiers left to join the fight. And suddenly, everything was normal again.

The war came to Tilsit for just a few days. And then we had peace. It was a peaceful, normal July—a normal summer vacation!

Gertrud's grade school

It's not that I hated school. But I didn't always like it. There were too many people and too much sitting!

Mama and Papa called me *Troddel* as much as they called me Gertrud. In German, a *troddel* is like a **pom-pom**. You know, it is something that is always bouncing up and down.

My cousin Bruno called me Weasel. That's because everyone on his soccer team had an animal nickname. I was the only girl on that team. And I was so good at slipping in and out with the ball that they called me Weasel! I loved that name.

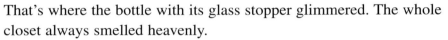

My sister, Eva, called me a baby. Eva was eight years older than I was. She thought being 18 was *so* grown-up.

"Gertrud!" Eva hollered.

Gertrud

Uh-oh. I smelled Eva's perfume. She must have opened the linen closet. That's where the bottle with its glass stopper glimmered. The whole closet always smelled heavenly.

"Have you been using my perfume again?" she demanded.

"No!" I said. "And I never have."

Eva thrust the bottle toward me. "I haven't used it. So why is there less?"

"I don't know!" I snapped.

She looked hard at me. "You're lying!" Eva growled.

"You're mean!" I cried.

"Your fighting will be the death of me!" Mama yelled from the kitchen.

My heart froze. What if Mama was right?

Mama wasn't young like the mothers some kids had. What if she got so upset, she had a heart attack? Old people can die. They can. They can.

I stomped away. Eva had started it. She started everything. But how could I tell Mama? Mama said fighting . . .

I ran outside, across the yard to Heta's. She was my best friend.

Heta answered the door. I whispered, "Is your father still mad at me for ringing doorbells and running?"

Heta slipped outside the apartment. "Not so much. But we'd better do something quiet today."

I guessed that meant we shouldn't follow the ice wagon, picking up dropped chunks. "I know!" I said. "Let's dress up and act out a fairy tale for the little kids!"

We ran to find the other girls. There were seven of us in the four buildings—Heta, Hannelore, Lieselotte, Gretel, Inge Samland, Inge Bauer, and me. We were all about the same age. We did lots of things together. We jumped rope or played hopscotch or ball.

**Lieselotte** (Lee-sa-LOT-a), **Inge** (ING-a), and **Hannelore** (Han-a-LOR-a) are German names.

That afternoon, though, we gathered crepe paper, ribbons, needles, and thread. We sat in the backyard and sewed paper costumes. Some boys from the buildings wandered over.

"What are these?" One boy ran his fingers under Lieselotte's fairy wings. "Bird wings?" he sneered.

"Or angel wings?" His friend's voice wasn't any nicer. "You don't look like angels to me."

They started fingering all the costumes. Then I heard something rip.

"Stop it!" I stood up. My knees shook a little.

"Who's going to make us?" The first boy grinned. "You little angels?"

front row, left to right: Hannelore, Lieselotte, Inge S.; back row, left to right: Inge B., Gertrud, Heta, and Gretel

11

"Look!" Another boy held Gretel's paper gown to his shoulders. "I'm an angel too!"

The boys laughed and grabbed more costumes.

"Gertrud, do something," Heta hissed.

"Get out of here," I said loudly. "We weren't bothering you."

The boys twirled with their skirts and wings. Inge and Inge tried to slap them away.

"Gertrud," Heta pleaded.

I punched the first boy with my fist.

He was mad now. I could tell. I could also tell he didn't want to hit a girl.

"Get out of here!" I warned. He shoved me down—hard. I scrambled up and hit him again. I used both fists this time, one after the other. I hit him again and again and again.

I heard the girls shrieking and the boys yelling. I was so scared, I couldn't breathe. But I was too mad to care. We were right! They had no business treating us that way! My hands hurt from hitting. My arms hurt from being punched. But I would not stop. Not until they left.

They didn't leave quietly. They yelled, strutted, and jeered as they walked away. That way it looked like *they* wanted to leave. Panting, I watched until I was sure they were gone.

"Oh, Gertrud." Heta was crying. "Your nose is bleeding."

I wiped my arm under my nose and looked. Sure enough, it was bleeding.

The other girls crowded around and fussed over me.

"Where were you five minutes ago?" I asked.

My dress was a mess. I trudged inside to clean up. When Eva saw me, she rolled her eyes.

Mama sighed. "At least we had peace for five minutes."

# Chapter 3

# August 1941

On rainy summer days, Heta and I cut paper-doll families from catalogs. We had pretty families with pretty names and ugly families with ugly names.

We had to get to the catalog before someone took the pages for toilet paper! I think the only place I knew that had real toilet paper was the movie theater. And, rain or shine, Heta and I loved going to the movies.

Movies were so big! They seemed as big as the world. Newspapers and radio told us about the world. But they didn't tell the news like the movies did. At the movies, you could see just how big everything was outside Tilsit.

The theater in Tilsit before World War II

We always saw some short newsreels first. Those were mostly about Hitler, our country's leader. He would be making a speech for millions of people, or saluting from a car in a huge parade.

Then we'd see a longer film. It was usually a war **documentary** about submarines or about farmers who learned to fly fighter planes. We saw lots of movies—never just one. But the shorter films were just something to sit through until we got to the big movie. Hopefully, it would be one starring Zarah Leander!

Zarah Leander was my favorite movie star. She was so beautiful! She would sing with her smoky voice and look at us with her smoky eyes. My favorite film was *Die Grosse Liebe*. It was a war story, of course. Zarah Leander was in love with an officer, and she was sure he would be killed in battle.

**Die Grosse Liebe** (dee GROH-suh LEE-buh) is German for "The Great Love."

Heta and I went to the movies even when we didn't know what movie was playing. We just loved the movies—except for one. I don't remember its name. But I remember the movie. And I wish I could forget it.

It started out fine. It was almost like *Die Grosse Liebe*, a love story and a war story. But in this movie, Polish people captured a group of Germans and put them all in a basement. The crowded Germans watched the feet of the Polish as they walked to the basement window.

14

Then a machine gun pointed in the window. The Germans ran toward the gun. That way the bullets would fly across the basement and hit the empty wall. But the barrel jerked down, straight at the Germans' heads.

One German man shoved the gun up away from the crowd just as it started blasting. His arms shook with the effort of holding this gun as it fired and fired and fired. His grip got weaker. He struggled to hold on. The others just stared. They were too terrified to move.

Finally, it stopped. The man tried to hold the gun one second more. He just wanted to be sure. But he couldn't.

His hands dropped. They were nothing but blood. The heat of the gun barrel had burned his flesh away.

I barely saw the lovers kissing at the movie's end. In my mind, I kept seeing those hands. Leaving the theater and walking Heta home, those hands followed me. Those mangled, bloody, black hands.

Maybe that's why Germany had attacked Poland two years before, I thought. We had to protect those Germans living in Poland.

We had won that war in just two weeks! Germans didn't live in Poland anymore. That's because there was no Poland now. Germany and Russia had split it.

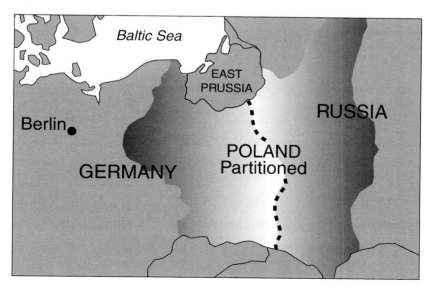

Polish people lived in Germany now. They worked for us, building Germany to what it had been years before.

My uncle had a Polish worker on his farm. There was a building, like a **barracks**, down the street from our apartment. It was full of Polish people. Usually, we ignored them. But that day, when I saw some Poles cleaning the park, all I could think of was the movie.

Heta and I passed a Polish woman, who was raking the grass. I didn't really look at her. But I said in a good loud voice, *"Polski!"*

We kept walking. But I turned and walked backwards.

"Polski!" I was louder this time.

Then Heta started chanting. "Polski! Polski!"

The woman didn't raise her head. Just her eyes.

"Polski! Polski!" we taunted.

The woman raised her rake and took a step.

Stupid woman, I thought. She wouldn't dare come any farther.

"Polski! Polski!" Heta and I sang.

But the woman kept coming. Her head was up now, and she was holding tightly on to that rake. Her steps quickened. Heta screamed.

"Polski!" I shrieked one last time. Then we ran. Pavement punched my shoes all the way home. My feet pounded up the stairs.

Mama was there.

# September 1941

Mama and I were **soul mates**. Maybe Eva knew. Maybe that's why Eva and I were always at each other's throats.

"You're such a mama's baby," Eva would sneer. But Mama and I just loved the same things—sewing, gardening, stories, and books.

Mama was a marvelous **seamstress**. She made all of our clothes. She'd sew for the relatives—neighbors, too, if they paid her. She was always busy in November and December. That was Christmastime, you know.

I'd sit in front of her sewing machine in the early winter dark. Sometimes, I'd sing carols in time to her feet pumping the machine. She'd sing with me. Candlelight flashed from the needle and her smile.

I learned to sew from Mama. I even made money by mending Eva's stockings!

Silk for stockings was hard to get because of the war. So were lots of things. We couldn't get imports from other countries. So Eva paid me to fix her old stockings. Her secretary's job took more hours than school. She was glad to pay me a penny or two for small holes and a nickel or dime for big ones. Sometimes we argued about price.

17

But I could tell by her face when I'd done a good job.

Mama's face was even better. I remember the proud look I saw when I finished a beautiful dress for one of my two dolls.

Best of all was making Mama laugh. She laughed until the tears rolled when I put doll dresses on Peter, our cat.

Peter was such a good cat! He'd let me slide dresses over his sleek black head. His little white feet looked like booties. Then I'd button him up and send him off. I knew when he'd found Mama by the squeals of laughter.

Mama and Gertrud

While Mama and I sewed together, we talked. We talked almost all the time. On summer nights, when Papa's tugboat stayed out on the river, Mama and I would lie on her bed and take imaginary journeys. We'd tell each other stories about what we saw on the way.

"Look out this side of the train!" Mama would point at the ceiling. "Do you see that fabulous bird?"

"I missed it!" I'd lean over. "Tell me about it." And she would.

Sometimes, she told me true stories that were just as strange.

Once when I was small, I pointed at the big photograph over our sofa. "Is this when you and Papa got married?" I asked.

"About that time," Mama said.

"Why is Grandma lying down in the picture?"

"Because she's dead," Mama said. Then Mama told me the story.

When Mama and Papa were young, there weren't any jobs in Germany. The factories had closed. People had no money for food. The towns and woods were full of homeless people.

18

Papa and Mama were in love then. But they waited to marry. They hoped things would get better.

But things got worse. Grandma died. Papa and Grandpa had no one to care for them. So Mama married Papa. It was sooner than they'd planned.

Mama and Papa started out with nothing. The family didn't even pose for wedding pictures. Instead, everyone gathered behind Grandma's coffin for a funeral picture!

That picture had been by the sofa for as long as I could remember. But even with Mama and Papa in it, it seemed like a whole different world. I couldn't imagine not having money for food, Papa without a job, homeless people.

Gertrud's parents in 1912

"I've never seen homeless people," I told Mama. "We can always get food at the grocery—even now with **war rations**. And Papa's boat always has work—and pay. There are rich people we have to nod to on the street. Lots of them even have cars!"

"Things changed when you were two," Mama explained. "That's when Hitler took over."

I knew that from school. I knew Hitler got German factories running again. People had places to work. They could buy food and houses. Our teachers said Hitler saved us.

Mama said it now too. "You have to hand it to Hitler."

Then she lowered her voice. "But I don't like a lot of what he's doing now. Changing our flag. Sending boys to war. Wanting people to say *Heil, Hitler!* instead of *Guten Tag!*"

I walked closer to hear. The weather was warm. Our windows were open. And Mama didn't want anyone else to hear. People might call the police if they heard Mama say she didn't like something about Hitler. Mama could go to jail. Or—or—somewhere worse.

Mama complained about that too.

"Imagine. Arresting someone for having a thought!" she muttered.

I didn't understand Mama sometimes. Didn't every country in the world have laws about what you could say? I'd never heard of any place different.

And, different or not, no place could be better. We'd learned that at school too. Germany was best in the world. The best place. The best people. I believed that.

Why doesn't Mama? I wondered.

> **Heil** (hyl) is German for "hail" or "salute." It shows respect.
>
> **Guten Tag** (GOO-ten tahg) is German for "Good day."

# Chapter 5

# October 1941

One o'clock. Another school day was finally over! I ran past the barracks of war prisoners, checking the window where the dentist's chair was. Sometimes, prisoners sat there with their mouths open.

My shoes slipped in front of the new police station. The pavement there was so shiny and slick! Kids who had roller skates loved skating there.

Next my feet carried me past the huge old Catholic church. I skipped over the bridge beside it. The wood quivered under my feet.

Tilsit Police Station before World War II

Then I passed Bruno's boys' school, some apartments, a neighborhood grocery, several houses, and another little grocery. I finally reached our **stucco** apartments with their neat wooden fences and whispering, rustling trees. Then I saw our curtains. Clattering up our apartment stairs, I smelled lunch.

Uh-oh. Carrots, I thought. I'd rather starve than eat carrots.

I'd never told Mama, but I knew when I grew up and had my own farm, I would not even *grow* carrots.

I ate slowly, watching Mama. Finally, she left the room. I dumped my carrots back in the pot.

"I have to go!" I called. *"Jung Maedel* meets today!"

This was my first year in Jung Maedel. It was a group for girls. You had to be 10 years old to join. When a girl was 14, she'd advance to the *Bund Deutscher Madchen*. And at 18, she'd join *Glaube und Schoenheit*.

We wore uniforms for Jung Maedel. They were white blouses, dark skirts, and special black scarves to tie under our collars. I loved wearing a uniform. It made me feel *so* tall!

We met once a week after school. Sometimes we met on Saturdays for singing, games, and exercise. Later in the year, we were going to have a sportsfest. The fastest runners and best throwers would get medals.

Gertrud

**Jung Maedel** (yoong MAY-dell) is German for "Young Maiden."

**Bund Deutscher Madchen** (boond DOY-cher MAYD-chen) is German for "Union of German Maids."

**Glaube und Schoenheit** (GLAU-buh oond SHUHN-hyt) is German for "Faith and Beauty."

I wanted a medal more than anything. And I was a good runner. The thought of a medal almost made Jung Maedel worth the boring parts—almost.

My steps got slower as I neared the meeting place. The first thing we would do would be to sing the national anthem. Then we'd sing another song about Hitler. And we were supposed to salute the whole time by holding one arm straight out in front of us.

Try holding one arm out for ten minutes. Just try it! Your arm gets really tired. My arm started aching as I walked to Jung Maedel.

> **Die Fuhrerin**
> (dee FYOO-rer-in)
> is German for
> "the leaders."

Maybe, I thought, I'll just skip this week. I have a nickel. I could go to the bookstore and rent a book. No, I better not. I skipped last week, and *die Fuhrerin* sent girls to my house to remind me. I hated that.

I started jogging. Maybe I could get there early. If I could sit behind someone, I'd rest my saluting arm on her shoulder. And if I sat in the back row, no one could rest on me! I sprinted into the schoolroom where we met. I squeezed in beside Heta.

Heta started telling me about a new girl at her school. We went to different schools now. I'd chosen the harder school called high school. Heta picked grade school. That was already hard for her. We were so busy talking that I didn't see die Fuhrerin come in. Chairs scraped as everyone stood. The piano sounded. We raised our arms.

> **Deutschland, Deutschland, uber alles**
> (DOYTCH-lund, DOYTCH-lund, EUH-behr AH-less)
> is German for
> "Germany over all."

Oh, no, I groaned to myself. The girl in front of me had moved!

Sighing, I sang along.

*Deutschland,*

Heta nudged me. I saw how she held her right arm up with her left. I tried it. Now my left arm ached too.

We started the next song.

I sang faster. Heta looked puzzled. But she tried to keep up. Some girls nearby heard and sang faster too.

The whole room sounded confused. My group sang louder and faster. We were done first! Our arms slapped down to our sides.

Our leaders rolled their eyes. They were older girls who'd already gone through Jung Maedel. But they knew they would get our attention with what came next.

We were going to make toys! Christmas toys for poor little kids.

I'd never used a jigsaw before. Heta and I hurried to the table to look at the darling patterns.

"Look at the rocking horse!" I cried.

"And this goose with a bonnet!" Heta exclaimed.

We cut animal shapes out of wood, sanded them smooth, and painted them. Then we added a set of wheels. Next we attached a string so kids could pull the toys around.

The time flew that afternoon. Much too soon, it was time for a final salute.

"Heil, Hitler!" we shouted together.

All the way home, I thought of Christmas.

# Chapter 6

# December 1941

I was careful as I crunched home through the snow. I had just finished copying a Christmas poem in my very best handwriting at school. Now I was bringing the precious paper home to decorate.

I was sure I could get a good grade on this. I was good at penmanship and art. We would also be graded on memorizing. But I wasn't bad at that either. I still knew the poem I had memorized in first grade!

> *Dear Santa, what a frown I see,*
> *But you don't need to paddle me!*
> *I'll be good as good can be.*

Of course, my poem this year was much harder.

Parents loved this assignment. Mama was going to make me recite my poem for all the relatives we saw.

After supper, I started drawing some stars around the edge of my poem. Suddenly, I realized today was December 5. It was St. Nicholas Day!

I had to get my shoes polished and put them by the door. That night, St. Nicholas would come. He would leave surprises in the empty shoes—but only if you'd been good.

I was dressing the next morning when our apartment door slammed.

"Mama?"

No one answered.

"You know," Eva smiled down at her buttons, "I have a funny feeling there'll be sweet rolls for breakfast today."

When we got to the kitchen, Mama seemed out of breath. Peeking from a paper inside my shoe was poppyseed cake. It was my favorite, and it was still warm! It was just like those that the bakery in our building made.

After lunch, Mama and I went Christmas shopping.

"Look, Mama!" I pointed to a poster in a window. "The Christmas play this year is *Cinderella*!"

"How nice!" Mama took my hand. Every year, we went to the play together.

"And this year," I skipped as Mama walked, "there's another holiday play! An **operetta**. And Jung Maedel girls get in free! It's next Sunday morning, and—"

Tilsit street scene before World War II

"Sunday?" Mama stopped. "We have church."

"I know," I said. "But it's a special occasion, and—"

"This isn't the first time something like this has happened," Mama said. "It's as if these Jung Maedel people do not think much of church."

I really wanted to see this operetta. "Mama," I pleaded. "That's just how theater schedules are. Everyone knows church is important. We study church history at school, for Pete's sake. And our preacher is a **party man**! On Sundays, I see his big, black Nazi boots under his church robes!"

"I need some handkerchiefs for your father," Mama said, turning into a store. I knew from her voice that she wasn't going to talk about the play anymore right now.

We walked by table after table until Mama finally asked where the handkerchiefs were.

"We're out," the clerk said. "We won't have any for a while."

"No handkerchiefs?" Mama spoke sharply. "We can't get a simple thing like handkerchiefs? Poor Germany!"

The clerk's eyes widened. She leaned and whispered to another clerk. I heard the words. "Should we call?"

"Mama, let's go!" I pulled on her arm. I managed to drag her into a crowd.

Mama knew better than to complain about war shortages in public! She could get arrested—taken away. And we'd never hear of her again. The only safe place to complain was with family.

I sighed. As least Christmas meant plenty of relatives for Mama to talk to—at home.

But Christmas Eve was just for Mama, Papa, Eva, and me. We decorated the tree. Then we went to the crowded church. We sang in church, and we sang when we got home. We opened every present that night. I had wished so much that Papa would love the green glass ashtray from me. And he did!

The next day, we visited the relatives. Bruno and I were the only kids young enough to have poems to recite. I was a little nervous as I stood by *Tante* Ida's Christmas tree.

**Tante** (TAHN-tuh) is the German word for "aunt."

> *I've seen the Christ Child. He came from the glen.*
> *He carried a bundle, with presents within.*
> *No one knew what was in it but me. I could tell*
> *There were apples and nuts! I could tell from the smell!*

I was glad when that was over! But the rest could have gone on forever. Papa and Onkel Max told jokes, Mama and Tante Anna laughed. We ate candy, cookies, and cakes so big they didn't fit in an oven. Tante paid the bakery to bake them.

Mama, Papa, Eva, and I talked and laughed as we walked home. Our apartment still smelled like our lunchtime feast of roast goose, apple stuffing, red cabbage, and boiled potatoes. The leftovers were wonderful! But I was sure to save room for a special treat—Jell-O! My favorite flavor, **woodruff**, tasted like the forest smells. And Mama made vanilla sauce to pour over it. Everything was so good, Papa even forgot to turn on the news. I licked my spoon and listened to Peter purring on my lap.

Everything was perfect.

# Chapter 7

# April 20, 1943

I was almost ready for bed when Eva got home. Her clothes smelled like the fresh spring night. She'd missed the radio news. So Mama and I told her about it while she washed up. As we talked, the sirens started.

"This is an odd hour for sirens." Eva said. She reached for the soap. No one really paid attention to sirens anymore. But we did pay attention to the next sound.

The sound burst into the room like a living thing. It roared so loud and so deep that the floors shook. A bomb had hit. And it had hit close by.

The sirens kept screaming.

We scrambled for the cellar. Clattering down the dark stairs, Mama gripped my hand. She squeezed my fingers until they hurt.

Another bomb cracked the air as we found an empty bench in the laundry room. Someone from the building had a candle. I couldn't remember how long it had been since we'd gone to the basement. I wasn't quite 10 then. I was almost 12 now. It had been two years—two whole years.

Why did this seem so familiar?

I looked around at the faces. In the flickering candlelight, everyone's face looked black and white, like a film. It was like a movie about Germans packed into a basement!

I clenched Mama's fingers.

Nobody talked because the bombs were so close. Planes whined. Bombs crashed. I thought I'd split each time one hit.

Don't be afraid, I told myself. Don't be afraid. Remember what they said two years ago. "If you hear the bomb, it won't hit you. If you can hear it, it's somewhere else."

*WEEEeeeeeeeeeee-oooooooooooooo!*

It's somewhere else. It's somewhere else.

*WEEEeeeeeeeeee-oooooooooooooo!*

Suddenly, there was nothing.

"Watch out when it's quiet," they had said. "When it's quiet, it's coming right at you."

My ears hurt from listening so hard. But the last bomb never dropped. The silence just went on.

Then the all clear finally blared. We went upstairs. But that silence followed us like an animal. Our own apartment felt strange. It was as if we'd been gone for weeks.

"Try to sleep now," Mama whispered. But I knew I would not sleep. Mama knew it too.

As soon as there was light outside, Mama was ready to go visiting. Her face was tight.

"Don't worry, Mama," I said as I took her hand. "Bruno and Tante Anna will be all right. Just like us."

Mama said nothing.

Outside, our building looked fine. As we started down the sidewalk, though, something was wrong. Trees were missing. A house was missing. A whole house I had walked by time and time again was gone. There was a huge mound of trash where the house ought to be. Now there were only splintered boards, broken glass, shreds of curtain, and twisted doors.

Mama and I moved slowly, picking our way around chunks blasted out to the sidewalk. I peeked back over my shoulder. The house had left a hole in the sky.

We passed another house I knew. It was caved in too. People were picking their way through the pile of rubble. They were clearing a space on the grass. They'd laid some big things in the cleared part of the yard. The things were long and covered with sheets.

I stopped. Bodies. Those were bodies in the yard.

I could make out the legs now. And heads. Noses. Foreheads. Chins. I knew I'd seen the faces under those sheets another day. I knew I'd said hello. They'd talked to me and waved. And now—

I didn't feel well. It must have been the smell of burning all around. That smell scraped my nose. My eyes hurt too. I could taste burning leaves, tires, and paint. I walked faster, hoping to get away from it.

Then I remembered where we were going.

Maybe Bruno and Tante Anna weren't all right. Maybe there were sheets in front of their house. Mama and I walked so fast that we were almost running.

The building was there! The apartment where Bruno lived was standing tall. They had to be all right. They had to be!

But Mama and I didn't slow down until we saw their faces. Mama took her sister's hand. Bruno and I let them stand there a minute.

Then we set out for Onkel Max's.

Mama cried out when she saw it. The house had taken a direct hit. The barn was burned to the ground. But then we saw Onkel Max—and Tante Ida.

"We lost some horses," he said. "But we can still live in half the house."

Mama stood a long time, looking at the wreckage.

"How can he do this to us?" she said under her breath.

I thought she meant the Russian ruler until Tante Anna said, "Hush! You want someone to hear you?"

# Chapter 8

# January 1944

After the big bombing, Tilsit went crazy getting ready for the next attack. Our white apartments were spray-painted green. So were most other white buildings in town. The green buildings were harder to see from enemy planes—day or night.

We'd cleaned out the attic so that if a bomb did hit, there would be less stuff to catch fire. Brick walls shaped like Ls guarded our basement windows. Extra poles braced the basement ceiling.

A big hole was punched in our shelter-room wall. The hole connected our shelter with the other half of the building. Then if something happened to the other side, the people living there could crawl to our shelter. Or if something happened to our side . . .

But nothing was going to happen. Since that one big attack, there had been nothing. Nine months—nothing. Almost a year!

The sirens went off as I got home from ice-skating. Papa was just getting home from breaking ice on the river with his boat.

Mama smiled as we came in. No one paid attention to the sirens. We hadn't for weeks. Nothing ever came of it now.

After supper, Papa winked. "I have to practice my music," he said. Then he sat down at the radio. "This is the only instrument I play!" he laughed.

He cocked his head, twisting the dial. Faint and faraway, we heard something. Was it German? We almost made sense of it when **static** took over.

Papa leaned back heavily. I sighed and tucked in the blackout curtains. These heavy shades kept light in so enemy planes couldn't see us.

I petted the cat and put coal in the room's heater. Then I switched on a lamp so I could do my homework.

Papa finally found a news special on the radio. It was all about a big Russian city we had just taken. But the program was suddenly interrupted.

"Attention! Attention!" A man screamed. "Here speaks The Man of the People!"

Papa bolted forward. Static chewed at the voice.

"Your leaders are lying to you about German loss—*sssssss*—" The newscast struggled to drown him out.

"They say just three planes—*sssssssss*—*ssss*—*ssss*—lost in Leningrad last night. But forty planes—*ssssssssssss*—*ssssssssssss*—*sssssssssss*—"

Papa twisted the dial. The radio squealed like a baby pig. The static cleared. The voice was gone.

"Troddel," Papa grinned, "lock the door. The Man of the People is out tonight!"

The Man was like a pirate—a radio pirate. He broke into German radio programs, saying he knew the truth about the war. Hundreds of our soldiers had been killed, he'd say. Or half our submarines were sunk. We didn't believe a word!

But it was still an adventure. We never knew when we would hear him. He had been gone for more than a week in silence this time. But once back, he usually showed up four or five short times in a night.

That's how it was with him. He never stayed on long. I didn't know if the **authorities** cut his signal, or if he only talked a short time so he'd be harder to track. We just knew that every time we heard him might be the last.

Of course, no one said a thing about him the next day at school. Not even when the teacher gave us a radio quiz.

"First question," *Fraulein* Kumerow said as her eyes swept the room. "Which German cities were attacked last night?"

I suddenly realized that I hadn't heard the news. I had been listening so hard for The Man of the People, I didn't really *listen* to the radio!

> **Fraulein**
> (FRAU-lyn)
> is German
> for "Miss."

I squinted at my paper. Hamburg, I wrote. Hamburg was always bombed. The same old cities were always bombed! Faraway cities that I'd never been to. Bremen, I wrote. Then I added Berlin and Dusseldorf.

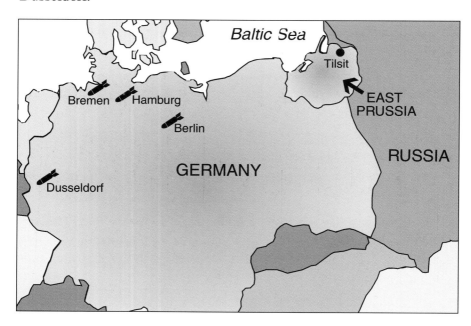

Sure enough, I passed the test. What a relief! I was wearing my new Jung Maedel uniform that day. I didn't want to goof up when I looked so important!

Just a few of us had been chosen to start training as future leaders. We had special meetings. We were learning how to be in charge of a Jung Maedel group someday.

Even better, we had brand-new, dark blue blazers instead of the short tan jackets like everyone else. We were the first to have them. And we got special tickets to buy them! We looked so much more important than people in the old group did.

That afternoon, I had to sit in the front row at the Jung Maedel meeting. But I didn't mind so much—not with my **elegant** uniform on. My arm got awfully tired during those songs. But I sang right on the beat. And I didn't even mind much when the leaders asked me to call on a couple of girls who missed the meeting. I used to hate doing that! But it's more fun to go places when you're dressed up and feeling important. And that's just how I felt.

**Chapter**

# Spring 1944

Tante Ida's mother was having a birthday party. She was already the oldest person I had ever seen!

We called her *Oma*. She acted like my real grandma. She was distant and grumpy. And she spent most of her time in bed. But everyone treated her with respect. Mama had even written a poem for her birthday. I'd memorized it. I would recite it at the party.

> **Oma** (OH-mah) is German for "Grandma."

On our way to the party, we stopped for Tante Anna and Bruno.

"Troddel, say Oma's poem for Tante Anna," Mama said.

"Then Tante Anna will have to hear it twice!" I protested.

"So?" Mama said. "This will be good practice."

"Mama! I don't need to practice!" I cried.

Mama's voice deepened. "It never hurts to practice. I want Tante Anna to hear my poem."

"It's Oma's poem!" I declared.

"Gertrud!" Mama thought I was being rude. But how can the truth be rude?

"I learned it for Oma." My voice was louder and higher than I wanted. "I'll say it at her party when it's time."

"Gertrud," Mama warned.

"I don't want to!" I shouted.

Mama slapped my face! No one breathed. Not Mama. Not Bruno or Tante Anna. Mama's eyes flashed angry, then sorry, then angry again. I didn't care. Slapping me like I—like I was a baby!

My cheek stung and my eyes burned. But I would not cry! I'd show her. I was a grown person who didn't need her coaching or nagging. I would say that poem perfectly, when I promised I would—not before!

"Well!" Tante Anna picked up her sweater. "Shouldn't we be going?" She kept chattering all the way there.

At the party, I sat by Tante Ida's good friends, *Herr* and *Frau* Schmidt. I was far away from Mama.

Herr Schmidt worked for the *Gestapo*. He arrested people who might

> **Herr** (hayr) is German for "Mister."
>
> **Frau** (frau) is German for "Mrs."

be dangerous to Germany. These people were like Mama. They didn't agree with everything Hitler did.

But Mama didn't hold it against Herr Schmidt. The government ordered him to do that job. If he said no, he'd be arrested himself.

"I've never seen the Gestapo take any Jews from town," Onkel Max told him. "Isn't that something you fellows do?"

I had never heard such a thing—taking Jews from town. That's why I liked listening to grown-ups when they talked.

Herr Schmidt told Onkel Max, "You've never seen us moving Jews because you aren't close to a Jewish neighborhood. And you're not near the train tracks where their transports leave from."

Wait, I thought. I had heard something about Jews on the news. Jewish people were Jewish first and Germans second. It was like if I lived in England, I would still be a German. That's why the Gestapo moved the Jews to places where they could live together. Germany would be stronger if everyone living here was German first.

"It seems like an odd job for an officer," said Tante Anna. "Moving people's furniture and things."

Herr Schmidt gave a half laugh. "They leave their furniture."

"Not when *you're* working," Frau Schmidt said, teasing her husband.

"That was only once!" he protested.

"Tell the story," she prodded.

Herr Schmidt sighed. "I was moving a group of Jews. An old woman begged to take her sewing machine. I told her the rules. Only clothes. What they could carry. But she said she could carry the machine. She would leave everything else. She said the machine would take care of her in her new home. And the look on her face . . ." His eyes went far away. Then he closed them and shrugged. "So I let her."

Just for a moment, I thought of Mama. What if she was evacuated for something she said? I wondered if she would beg to take her sewing machine. I knew she'd want to. But I knew she would never beg. Neither would I.

We should have been happy walking home. Everyone had loved Mama's poem. But I was still mad at her. I could still feel her slap glowing red across my face.

The apartment building where Gertrud's family lived

As Mama unlocked our apartment, the door across the hall opened. My heart turned a cartwheel.

"Fraulein Motzkus!" I shouted.

Our neighbor, Fraulein Motzkus, was home from the **front**. She was a nurse, just like in the movies. We looked after her apartment when she was gone. She almost never came home. But when she did, she talked to me like an equal—like a grown-up. And Fraulein Motzkus let me help her with cooking and cleaning. Mama never did.

"Go play," Mama would say when she had work. She treated me as if I were a baby.

"Gertrud!" Fraulein's smile glowed on her rosy cheeks. "Would you like to help me cook supper?"

I think that's when I decided to become a nurse, just like Fraulein Motzkus.

## Chapter

# Summer 1944

Heta and I had big, big plans for this year's summer vacation. After all, we were 13 now. It was about time we got out on our own a little—without grown-ups! So, for our first big adventure, we decided to go camping alone. It would just be the two of us.

I could hardly wait! We would stay at the *laube*.

My family rented a fenced-in plot at the public gardens just outside of town. There were berry bushes and apple trees. We grew flowers and

**Laube** (LAU-buh) is German for "cabin."

vegetables. That's where the laube was. It was a little cabin where we kept tools. But the laube also had curtains and two canvas benches that folded out to make cots. It was perfect. There were things to eat and a place to sleep. And we could talk all night if we wanted!

Heta and I left after dinner one night, carrying pillows and blankets. A half hour later, puffing from the uphill hike, I unlocked the gate. Then I closed it behind us. We were alone in the garden.

We ran to the berry bushes. They were still warm from the day's sun. We ate and giggled until dark.

We finally crawled into our cots. I shivered as I pulled the blanket over my dress. It wasn't because I was cold. I was just so happy.

I thought Heta was asleep when she whispered, "Gertrud?"

"What?" I answered.

"What was that?" Heta asked.

"That whistling?" I asked. It did sound odd. "Just a bird, I guess."

"All right . . ." Heta's voice faded. Then it grew. "What's *that*?"

I didn't like that sound either. It was sort of fluttery and thumpy.

"What do bats sound like?" Heta's voice quavered.

"I don't know," I whispered.

There it was again.

"Do you hear scratching?" I asked.

"Something's trying to get in!" Heta sat up. "An animal!"

"What—what kind?" I stuttered.

"I don't care. I just want to go home!" Heta cried.

We threw our blankets and ran.

It'd taken half an hour to get to the cabin. In five minutes, we were halfway home. My legs were like Jell-O, but my feet kept pounding. The night air scraped my throat as I ran. It scraped so much that I couldn't even scream when the thing—the black thing—rose out of the ditch.

Heta gulped back a cry too.

It was a shadow, huge and black. Was it a man? Or a bear? Was it coming toward us?

We didn't wait to see.

We finally got to my building. But it was black.

"Do you—have—a key?" Heta puffed.

I shook my head and started pounding on the downstairs door. "Mama!" I called. "Mama! Let us in!"

It must have been past midnight when we finally fell asleep in my bed.

Eva teased us the next day. But that was all right. What an adventure we'd had! And Heta and I were positive that our next plan couldn't fail.

We decided to visit Heta's grandma, who lived in the forest across the River Memel. I loved the thought of riding the train, just the two of us.

I pictured us at her grandma's. I imagined a fairy-tale cottage. We'd pick berries in the woods. The sun would sift down around us.

I was so excited dreaming about it, I couldn't sleep the night before we left! But I finally drifted off.

Then the sirens blared. Oh well, I thought, and rolled back over.

Then a bomb hit. It had been close. My bed jumped halfway across the floor.

I stumbled to the basement. I couldn't think. How long had it been since Tilsit was hit? It had been Hitler's birthday. But it wasn't this year. It had been more than a year ago.

I remembered seeing the dead people. But that was so long ago. I thought it wouldn't happen again.

It won't be so bad this time, I thought. I sat tall beside Mama on the cold, hard bench. We're ready this time.

Think of the cement walls, I reminded myself. The camouflage paint. Windows boarded up. Bomb shelters all through town. Tilsit was ready.

A bomb hit close, rattling my teeth, elbows, and shins. It'll stop soon, I told myself. The Russians are just trying to scare us. It'll stop soon, I told myself as bomb after bomb after bomb hit.

It didn't stop until the darkness stopped. We climbed the stairs like old people that morning. We were as stiff as the cold, gray light. I thought of my bed waiting as I pushed open our door.

Aerial view of Tilsit prior to World War II

Almost every window was shattered. Out the window frame, I saw windows missing in every other building.

Mama cried out behind me as her eyes raced over the damage. We stood silent until I couldn't anymore.

"Oh, Mama," I wailed. "Now we can't go to Heta's grandma's!"

# Chapter 11

# July 25, 1944

Heta

But Mama wanted me to go.

"If Heta is still going to her grandma's, you go too," she said. "You'll be safe there."

I never thought about Mama being safe. All I could think about was that sweet, small cottage in the woods. I thought about that while I picked up bits of glass. And I thought about that while I swept up plaster dust and chunks that had shaken off our walls.

Right after lunch, Heta and I took a little train ride to her grandma's. It was everything Heta had promised. Her grandmother lived in this huge forest. And there were blueberries! We ate and ate. Then we walked together under the trees. It seemed like a dream, but it was better. Fresh air and trees are so *real*. Now the night before seemed like a dream—dark, distant, and muddled.

Cool country air filled our bedroom that night. Heta and I could hear crickets and birds. And we could hear the planes. The planes were headed toward Tilsit.

We tried to look out the window, but the trees blocked our view. We heard bombs thunder against the earth. The sky in the trees turned red. Tilsit was burning.

But what part of Tilsit? Our apartments? Our families? Were Heta and I alone now? Without parents? Without anyone?

We left as soon as we could the next morning. The train took so long going home! As we pulled into Tilsit, we saw bricks tumbled like waterfalls from buildings with no roofs. The whole town looked like a set of blocks some kids had built and then kicked down. And everywhere, fire and smoke burned our eyes and throats as we ran from the train. We ran so hard we couldn't think. We ran until we saw our apartments.

They were standing. Everyone must be all right. They must be . . .

I couldn't remember the last time I'd squeezed Mama as hard as I did then. She stroked my hair.

"Help me clean up," she said. "Then we'll get ready to go."

"Go?" I knew now what I should have known last night. Parents send their children away to be safe.

"Where?" I asked. "I don't want to go without you."

"We'll walk out into the fields tonight," Mama said. "Together. They don't bomb the farms, just cities and harbors. We'll find a barn or a field to sleep in."

I had always wanted to sleep under the stars. But this was not how I had imagined it.

Mama, Eva, Tante Anna, Bruno, and I set out before dark. The roads were packed with people like us. All carried little bags with just enough for one night. We had our birth certificates and other important papers we wouldn't want burned.

We passed a farm already full of people. Its fields were dotted with blankets. And then we passed another and another.

At last, we found a barn. The hay was soft, but we didn't sleep. We looked out over the fields that night, watching Tilsit burn.

We cleaned up again the next day and the next. It wasn't so bad after that. All the windows had already been broken. We didn't bother putting in new glass. It would just get broken again. Besides, we couldn't buy glass anywhere. We used boards, if we could get them, to cover the windows. I pulled the blackout shades to hide them. At least the shades looked normal.

At night, everyone left home to sleep somewhere else. In the morning, we'd come home and clean up. Then Eva would go to work in her office, and Mama and I would go to the garden.

The garden was like another world. The little laube stood like always. The trees and birds were undisturbed. I could smell flowers and apples—no rubble. No fires. I pretended the artillery that I heard was only thunder.

It was harder to pretend back in town. People were leaving Tilsit every day. "We know people in Saxony," they would say, or "We have relatives in Langenau." The newspapers and radio encouraged them to go.

"It's only for a little while," the news said. "Hitler's scientists are working on a secret weapon. It will be strong enough to finish the war."

We knew it must be true. Just one month ago, Germany fired a robot bomb all the way across the sea. Think of it! A bomb that flew from here to London—alone! There was nothing like the V-1 bomb anyplace else. And the news said the V-2 was almost done. And there might even be a V-3. If we could just hang on, the war would be over. If we could just hang on, we could all go home.

It won't be long, we told ourselves as the bombs dropped in July.

Any day now, we told one another as Tilsit burned in August.

Any day now . . . any day now . . .

Chapter

# September 1944

It was September, but I wasn't in school. There weren't enough kids left in Tilsit. That's why I was home the morning a letter came for Mama.

"Gertrud," she said. Her eyes never left the words. "Tante Grete needs us."

My heart froze. All this time, our family had been fine. No men drafted as soldiers. No one hurt or killed. But now . . .

"Did a bomb hit?" I asked. "Has somebody died?"

Mama turned. "It's the cows."

Cows? I trotted after Mama. "Tante Grete's never had cows."

"She doesn't know where they're from," Mama said, adding a dress to the bag with her nightgown. "But the Russian army is closer every day. Some farmers probably evacuated and just turned their animals loose.

"All Grete knows is there are cows near her house. And they are crying. They haven't been milked in days. Milk's building up inside them. If no one helps, they'll die a slow, horrible death."

I remembered, suddenly, cows here in Tilsit. Dead cows had washed onto the riverbanks. I'd thought that they had drowned— that there had been an accident. Now I wondered if they had died because people only thought about their own skins. The poor cows!

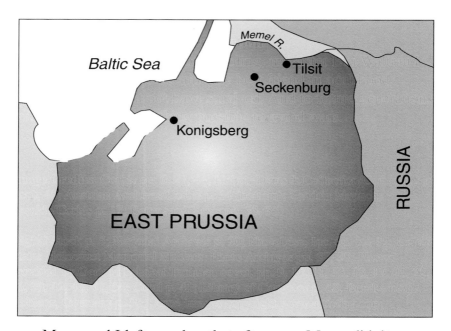

Mama and I left on a bus that afternoon. Mama didn't want to leave Papa and Eva. But she wanted me out of Tilsit. Bombs pounded down almost every night now. One had hit so close to Tante Anna's house that her whole roof caved in. Luckily, they weren't sleeping at home anymore. Neither were we. The last few nights, we'd slept at the office building where Papa got the orders for his boat. There was a **bunker** in the basement there.

Tante Grete lived in Seckenburg. When we arrived, I wondered if they even needed bunkers in Seckenburg. We were only ten miles from Tilsit, but Seckenburg was small. The Russians probably wouldn't waste a bomb on it.

The next morning, Tante Grete woke us early. Then she and Mama set off with a wagon full of rattling, empty milk cans.

"You stay," Mama told me. "You don't know anything about cows." So I sat the whole morning and into the afternoon. I was alone except for Tante Grete's old grumpy mama.

Maybe too much happened in Tilsit. But from what I could see, not enough was happening in Seckenburg.

Every time I heard a wagon, I hoped it was Mama. I lost count of how many wagons passed before Grete's wagon finally sloshed and clanged to the door.

"So much milking!" Mama let go of the wagon and stretched her fingers in front of her.

Tante Grete grinned. "Now we've got to do something to save all this milk! We'll make cheese and butter right after lunch."

At least that was something I could help with. Pumping the butter churn wasn't hard. Up—down. Up—down. Up—down.

We kept stirring the fresh cream until it thickened slowly to butter. When one arm ached, I switched to the other. Mama and Tante Grete filled big pans while I churned. They cooked the milk, curdled it, strained it, pressed it, and left it to age into cheese.

I looked around. The kitchen—the living room—the whole house was full of dairy products.

"Tante Grete, what will you do with all this?" I asked.

"Help me fill the wagon and you'll see." Grete strode to the pantry and started handing me loaves of bread, cheeses, butter, glasses, and pitchers of juice made from her berry bushes. I had to keep rearranging the wagon as she gave me more and more.

Finally Tante Grete said, "Gertrud, follow and make sure nothing falls out." Then she rattled the wagon to the roadside.

I saw a farmer's wagon not far down the road. There were three more a little beyond. Neighbors coming home, I supposed. The first had a huge load of hay, brimming over the sides of the wagon. But as the wagon came near, I saw it wasn't hay. It was chair legs and blankets. The cart was loaded with furniture and trunks. It was so full that the people were walking.

They were homeless because the Russians were coming. They had to leave their homes quickly.

They looked like a family—a man, a woman, a teenage boy, and a smaller girl. They walked heavily, as if they had been walking all day. They didn't talk, as if there was nothing to say. An old woman sat in a chair in the wagon. She glared down as the wagon rattled to a stop.

"Would you like some juice?" Tante Grete asked. She acted as if they were long lost friends. The boy nodded once. The girl reached out, smiling. The woman passed a glass to the grandma. The man drank, keeping his eyes on the fields that were far away from our eyes.

"I have bread," Grete said when the woman finished drinking. "Take two loaves. And cheese. And fresh milk too. A growing boy needs lots . . ."

The boy scowled as his mother pulled pots from the wagon for Grete and me to fill. I heard more wagons rumbling.

Then I looked up and saw the girl staring at me. She was as tall as I was. She was as old as I was.

The girl had looked smaller when she was far away. The war had seemed much smaller too—when it was far away.

# Chapter 13

# October 1944

After two weeks, Mama was even more worried about Papa than she was about the cows. So we came home. Mama kissed Papa and Eva. I hugged Peter. Then I ran across the yard to see Heta.

I knocked. No one answered. I knocked again.

"They're gone," said a voice. It was one of Heta's neighbors.

"Gone?" I asked.

Gertrud's parents

"Took everything with them," the woman said. "They won't be back."

I knew Heta might have to leave one day. But I thought we would at least say good-bye. I thought we would be able to write.

"Thank you." I sounded broken. I felt broken. But I did not want to go home. I would have to tell Mama what happened. And if I said it out loud, I'd cry.

We didn't go to the bunker at night anymore. Papa's tugboat was working near Tilsit now. The boat was anchored miles from town. We went out on his ship each night and slept until the attack. Then we would jump off the boat and crouch in the trenches with Papa's crew.

The trenches had been dug in the riverbank for the German soldiers. They would fight from there if the Russian army came. Until then, we used the trenches during air raids.

The dirt in the trenches was damp and cold on my legs. I would pull my nightshirt over my knees and lean my head against the dirt wall. I could see everything from there.

Searchlights sliced the night. So did Eva's eyes, chasing fighter planes above us. Shadows dropped on Mama's face. Bombs pounded the earth, making my ribs and heart ache. And no matter how many times we were trapped there, no matter how many times we escaped, I wondered every time if tonight was the night. If this would be the night a bomb hit so hard that the whole world would just stop.

"Ida," Papa said one morning. I could hear the artillery rumbling behind his voice. I heard it every hour of every day now. It never stopped.

"Ida," Papa said, "you've got to take Troddel and get out of here. The Russians are coming by land."

"And what about Eva?" Mama said.

"She's keeping books for the government," Papa replied. "She's got to stay. So do I. I'll look after her."

"And who'll look after you?" Mama asked.

Mama stopped folding clothes and just stood, looking down.

"Tilsit is our home," she said. Her voice was unsteady. "This is where our family is. Where would we go? We don't know anyone where it's safe."

"The government will find someone you can stay with," Papa said.

Mama pressed her lips together. She didn't want to go. I didn't want to either. I didn't care about the bombs. This was still our home.

Didn't those Russians realize that? They thought if they dropped enough bombs, we'd give up. Just like those stupid boys who came and tore up our costumes. They thought we'd crawl on our knees and say, "Please stop. Please stop the fighting."

Never.

The more they bombed us, the stronger our feelings against them grew. What had I ever done to the Russians? Or what had Mama ever done? Or Eva? Or Papa? We lived in Germany. It wasn't our fault we were born here. It wasn't our fault Hitler went to war. He didn't ask us. And we'd go to jail if we opposed him.

But we were still Germans. We couldn't help that. We couldn't help that these hills, these forests, and these rivers were home. We couldn't help that Germany was home to all of our memories. We couldn't help that every dream we had ever made took place at home.

We would always be Germans, no matter who Germany's leader was. And we did not want to leave.

But the government gave us no choice.

The next day, the order came. All women and children not needed by the government must leave Tilsit within a week. That meant Papa and Eva had to stay. Mama and I had to pack.

I tried to imagine where we were going—like I'd imagined when I was going to Heta's grandma's. But we'd never been to any cities west of us. We didn't know anyone there. We didn't know where we would find food or shelter.

I didn't know what to imagine.

I put my two dolls in the suitcase. They were big dolls, like real babies. I couldn't just leave them. At least I didn't have that many clothes to pack. And I could wear a lot of clothes at once to save suitcase room.

Mama was doing the same thing. She was filling her case with pots and pans. We knew the trains were going to be crowded, so we only took as much as we could carry.

I thought suddenly of the old Jewish woman Herr Schmidt had talked about.

Eva came to walk with us to the train station. She and Mama looked around, then started slowly down the stairs. As their footsteps got fainter, the sound of the artillery grew louder and louder.

I remembered when it used to be so far away.

I took one last look around our apartment. I heard something. Was it a bird? It sounded like crying.

It was crying.

Peter was in a tree outside. He was looking in the window, meowing. But I turned my back and ran after Mama.

The train station in Tilsit prior to World War II

# Glossary

**air-raid siren**    device to warn people of an approaching enemy attack by air

**antiaircraft**    designed to defend against air attack

**authority**    one in charge; government official

**barracks**    building or set of buildings used for lodging, especially for soldiers

**blackout**    period of darkness enforced as a precaution against air raids

**bunker**    shelter built to protect against bombs and explosions

**Communist**    following a belief, or a political policy, that elimates privately owned property and has commonly owned goods

**documentary**    short film that is factual

**elegant**    graceful and dignified

**front**    zone of conflict between armies

**Gestapo**    secret-police organization that employed underhanded and terrorist methods against persons suspected of disloyalty

**operetta**    romantic comic opera that includes songs and dancing

**party man**    person who follows the rules of an organization, often encouraging others to join

**Polski**    form of the word *Polish* that was used in a negative manner

**pom-pom**    a decorative ball or tuft used especially on clothing, caps, or costumes

"Youth Serve the Fuehrer" is the title of this German propaganda poster.

**propaganda**    information, rumors, or facts purposely spread to support a certain cause or idea or to damage a certain cause or idea

**seamstress**    woman whose occupation is sewing

**soul mate**    person whose moods, feelings, and such are suited to another

**static**    noise produced in a radio or television by natural or human disturbances

**stucco**    material made of portland cement, sand, and a small percentage of lime; applied to form a hard covering for exterior walls

**war ration**    amount of goods allowed civilians during wartime; usually food and gasoline

**woodruff**    small, sweet-scented herb found in Europe